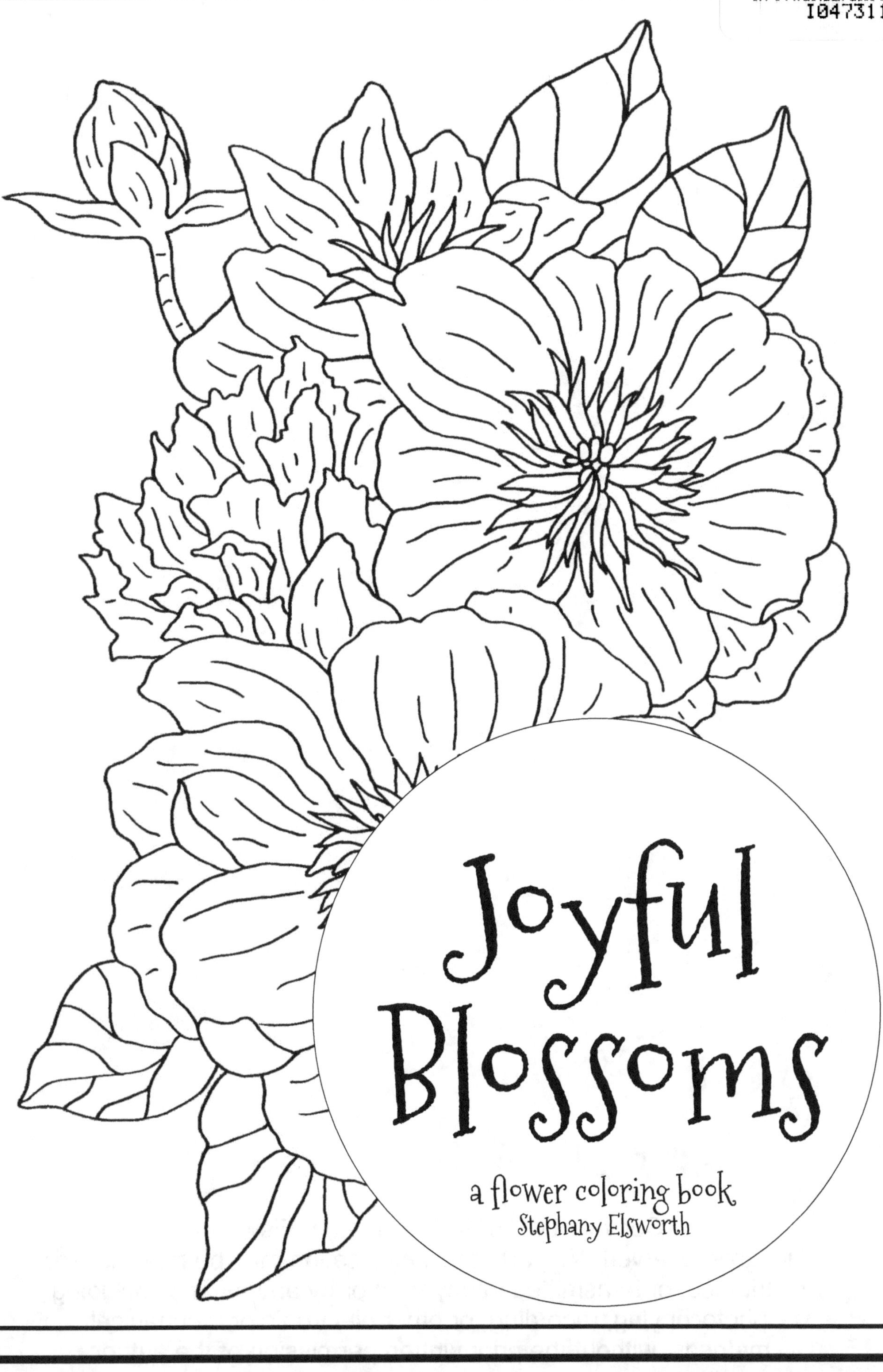

Joyful Blossoms

a flower coloring book

Stephany Elsworth

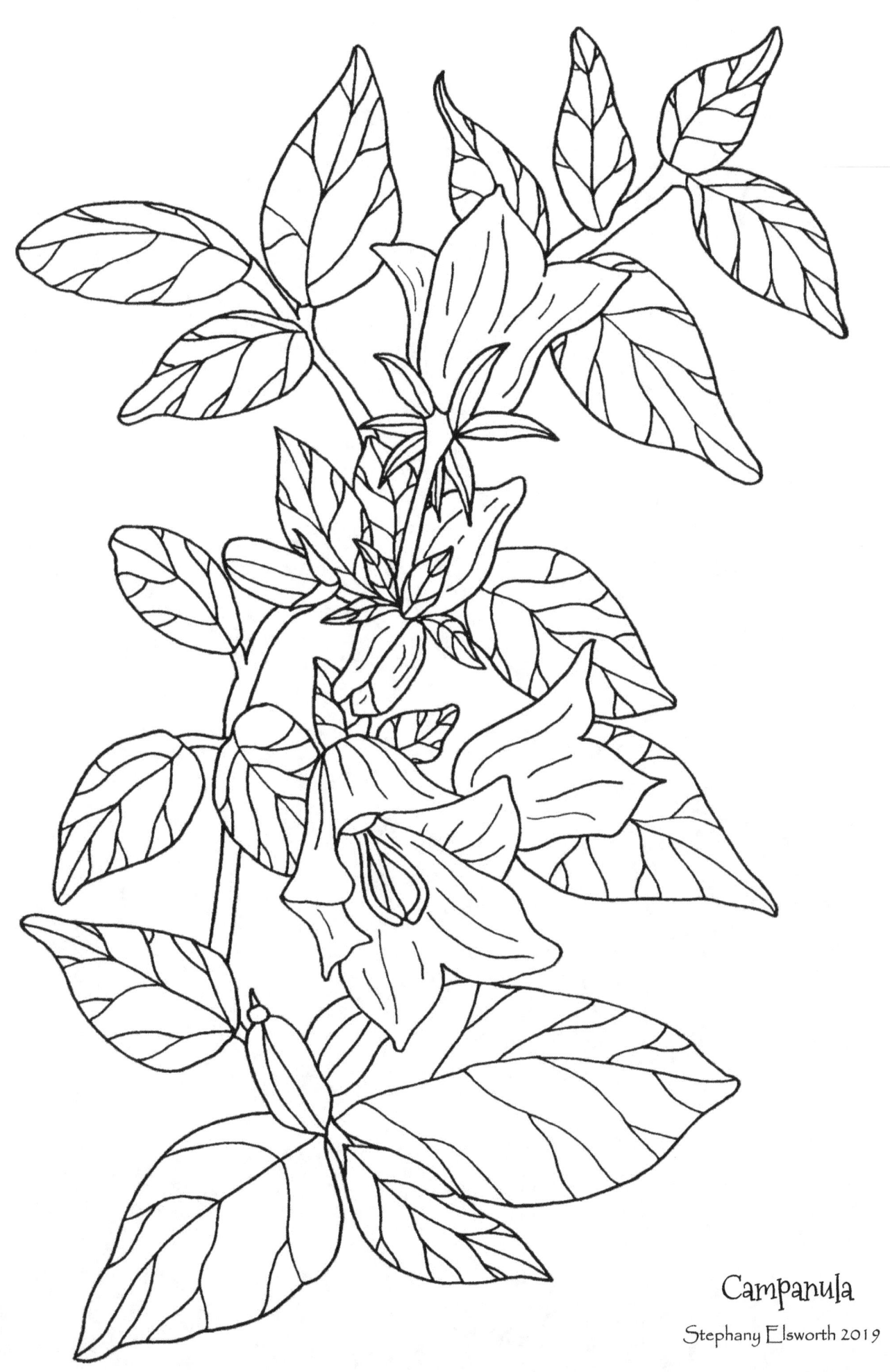

Campanula

Stephany Elsworth 2019

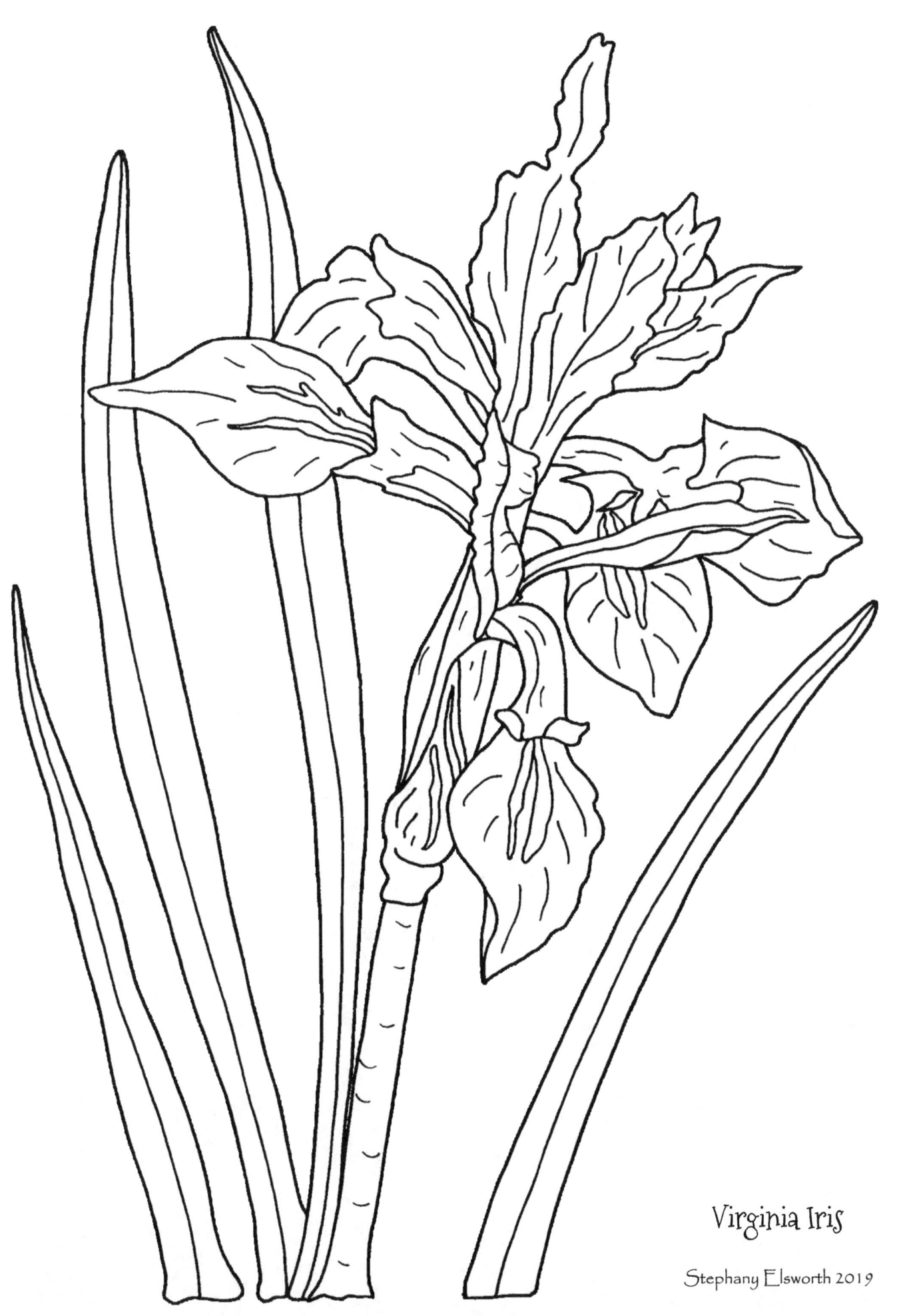

Virginia Iris

Stephany Elsworth 2019

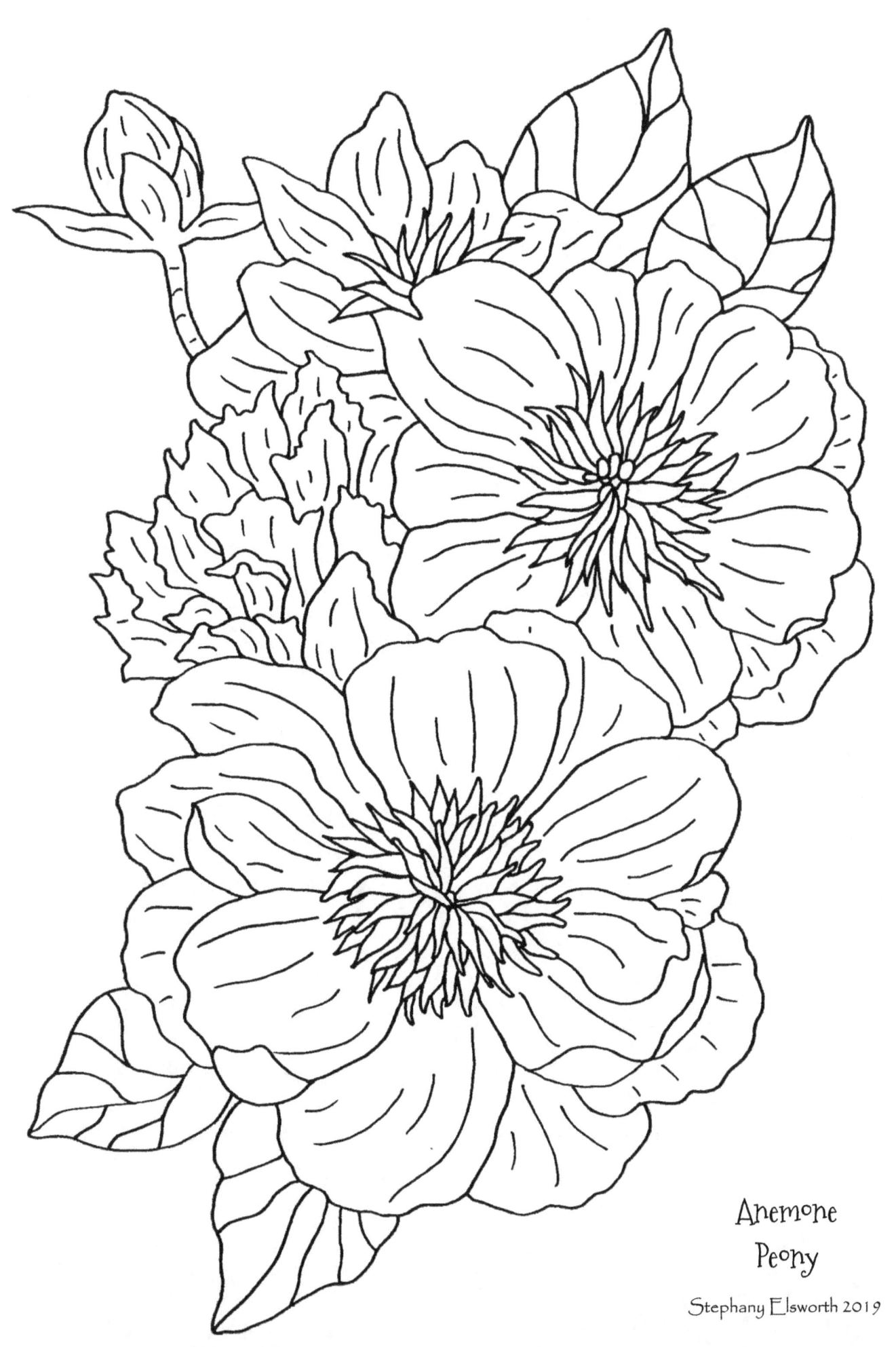

Anemone
Peony

Stephany Elsworth 2019

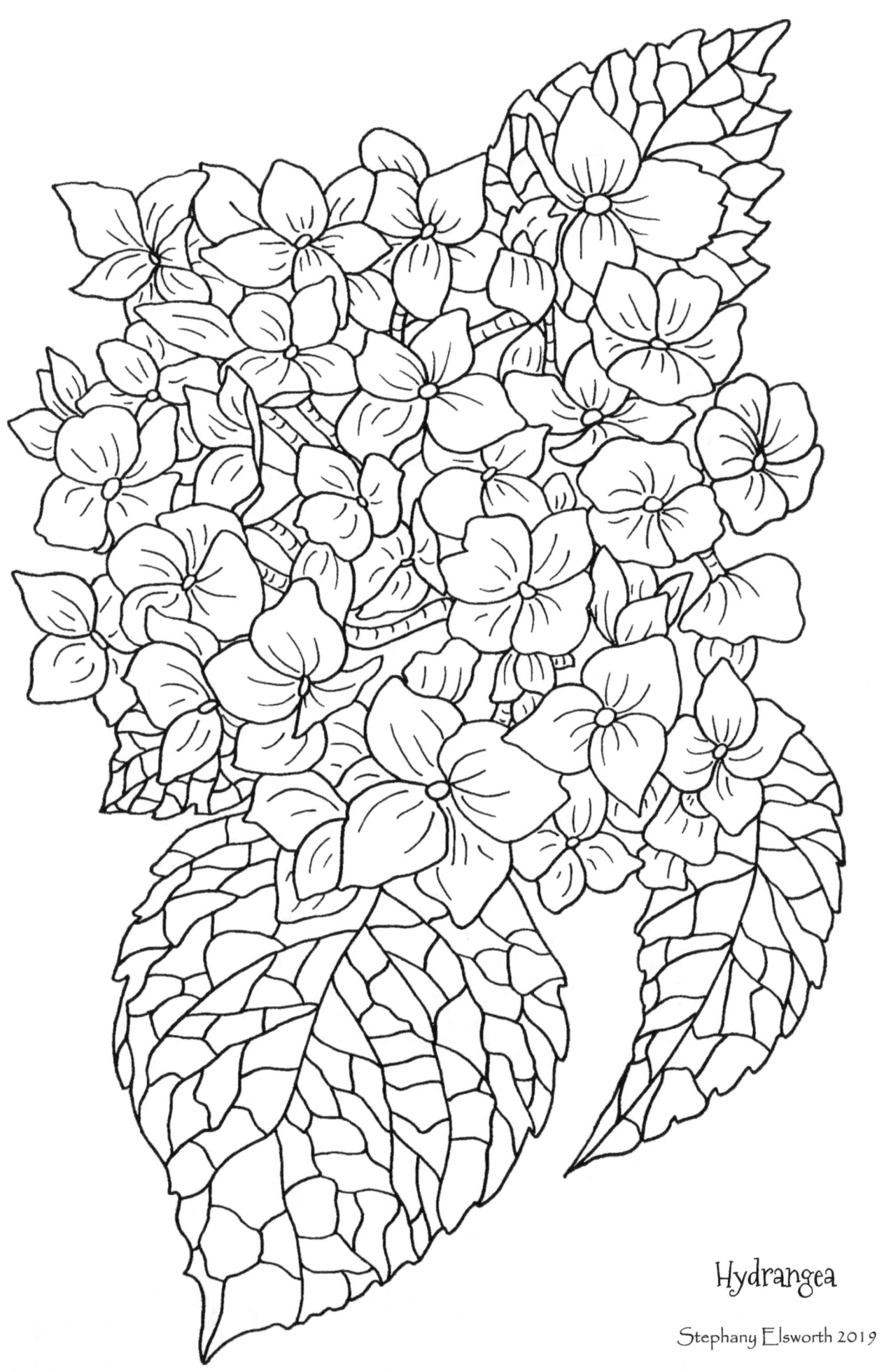

Hydrangea

Stephany Elsworth 2019

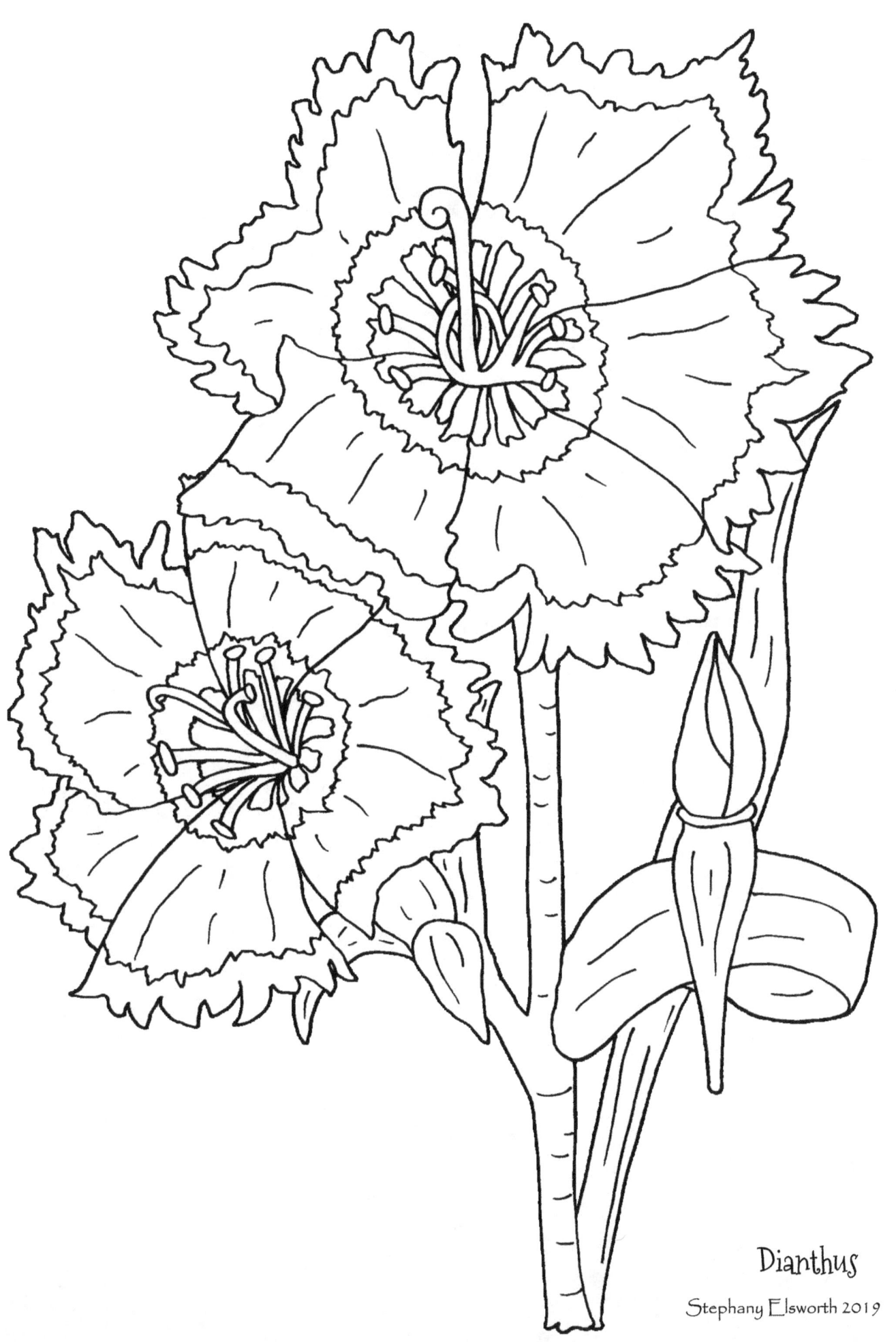

Dianthus

Stephany Elsworth 2019

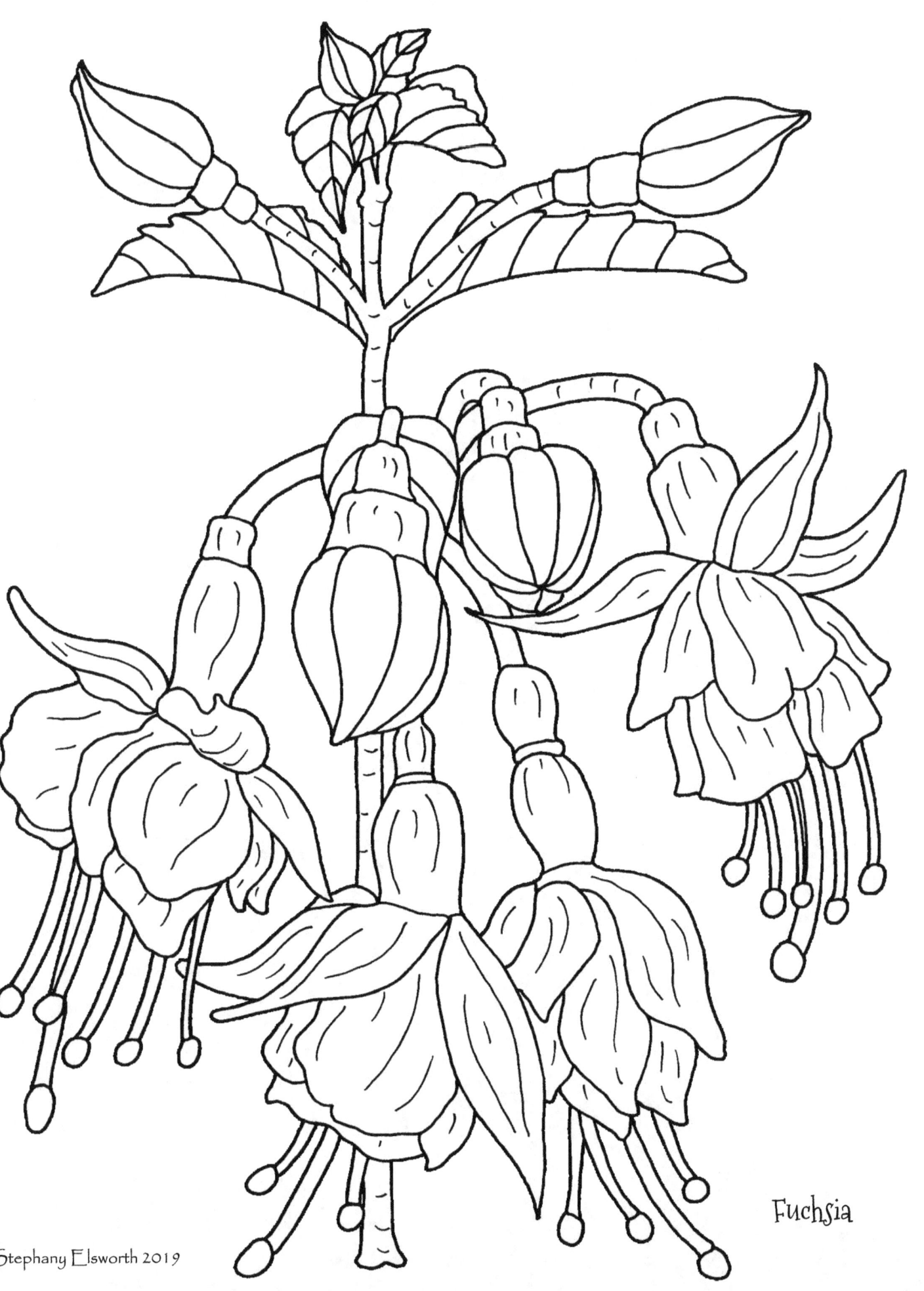

Stephany Elsworth 2019

Fuchsia

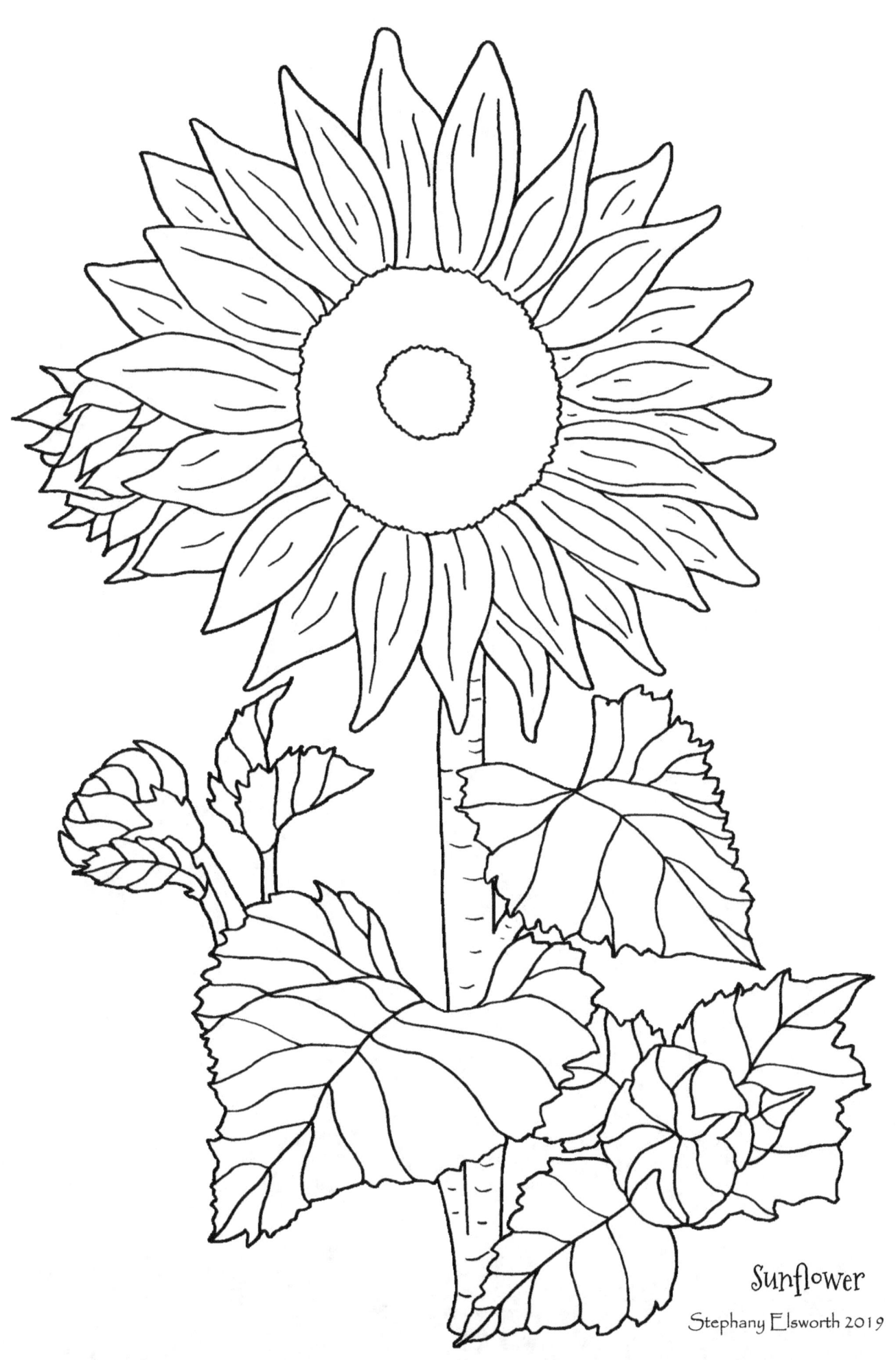

Sunflower

Stephany Elsworth 2019

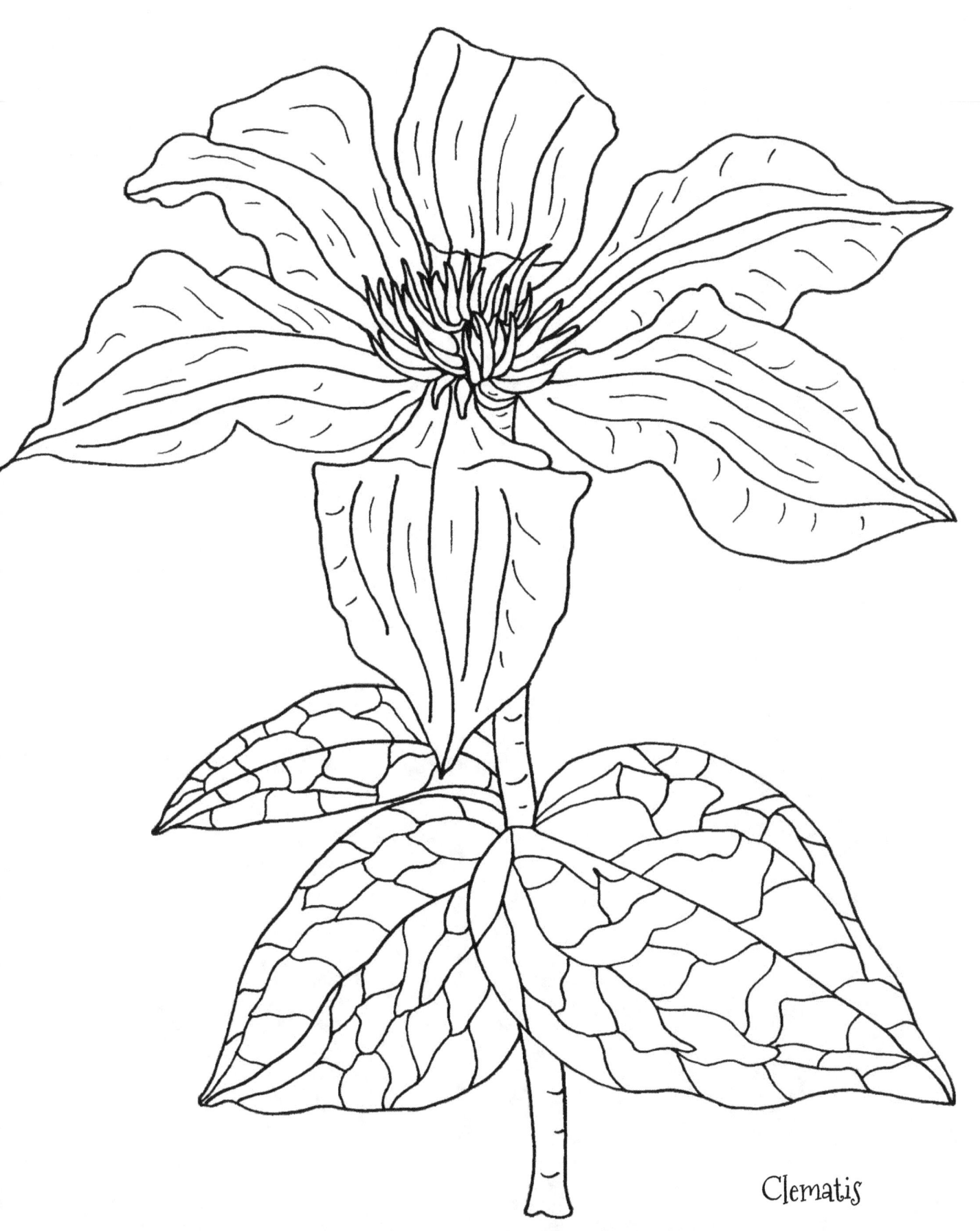

Clematis

Stephany Elsworth 2019

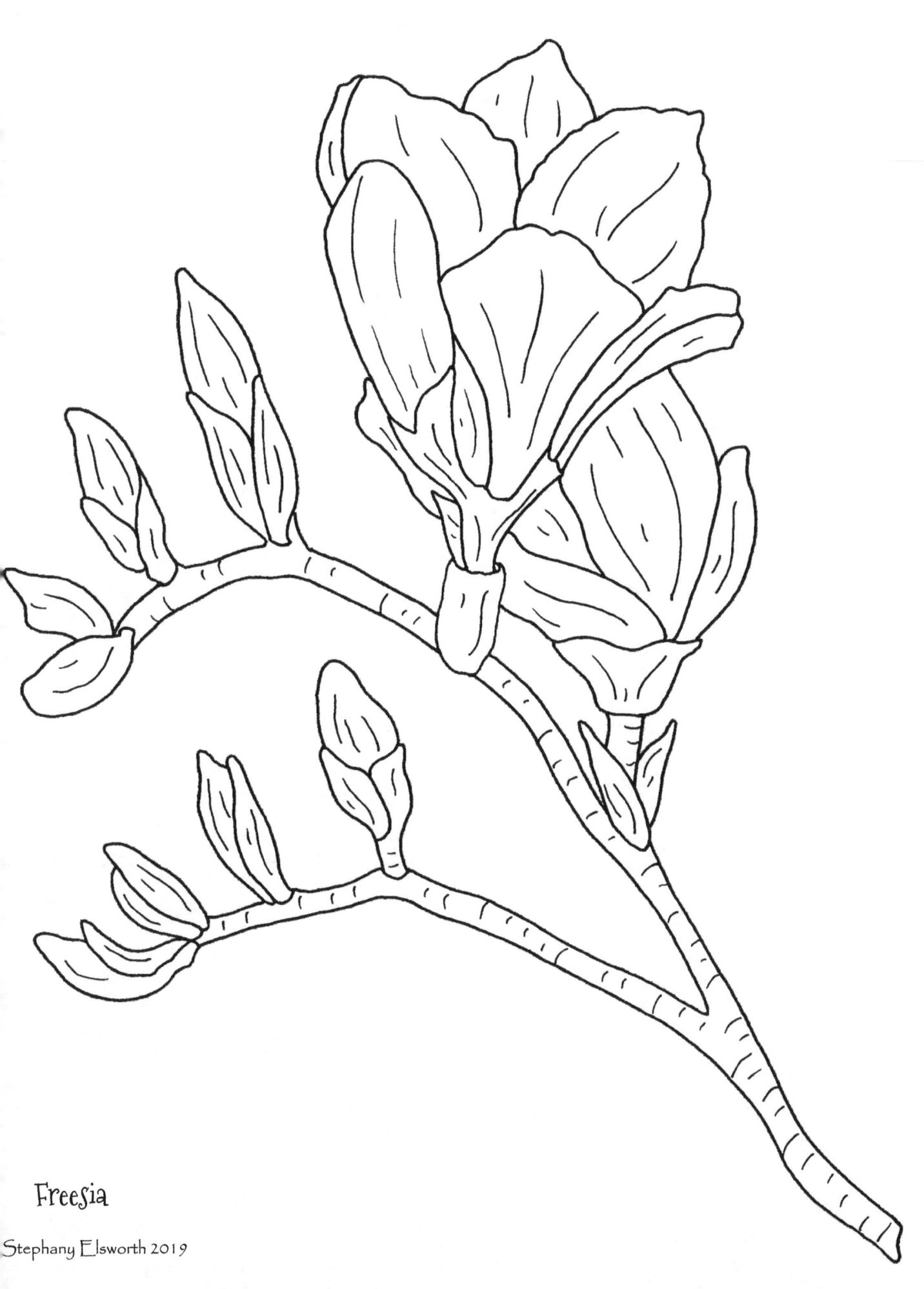

Freesia

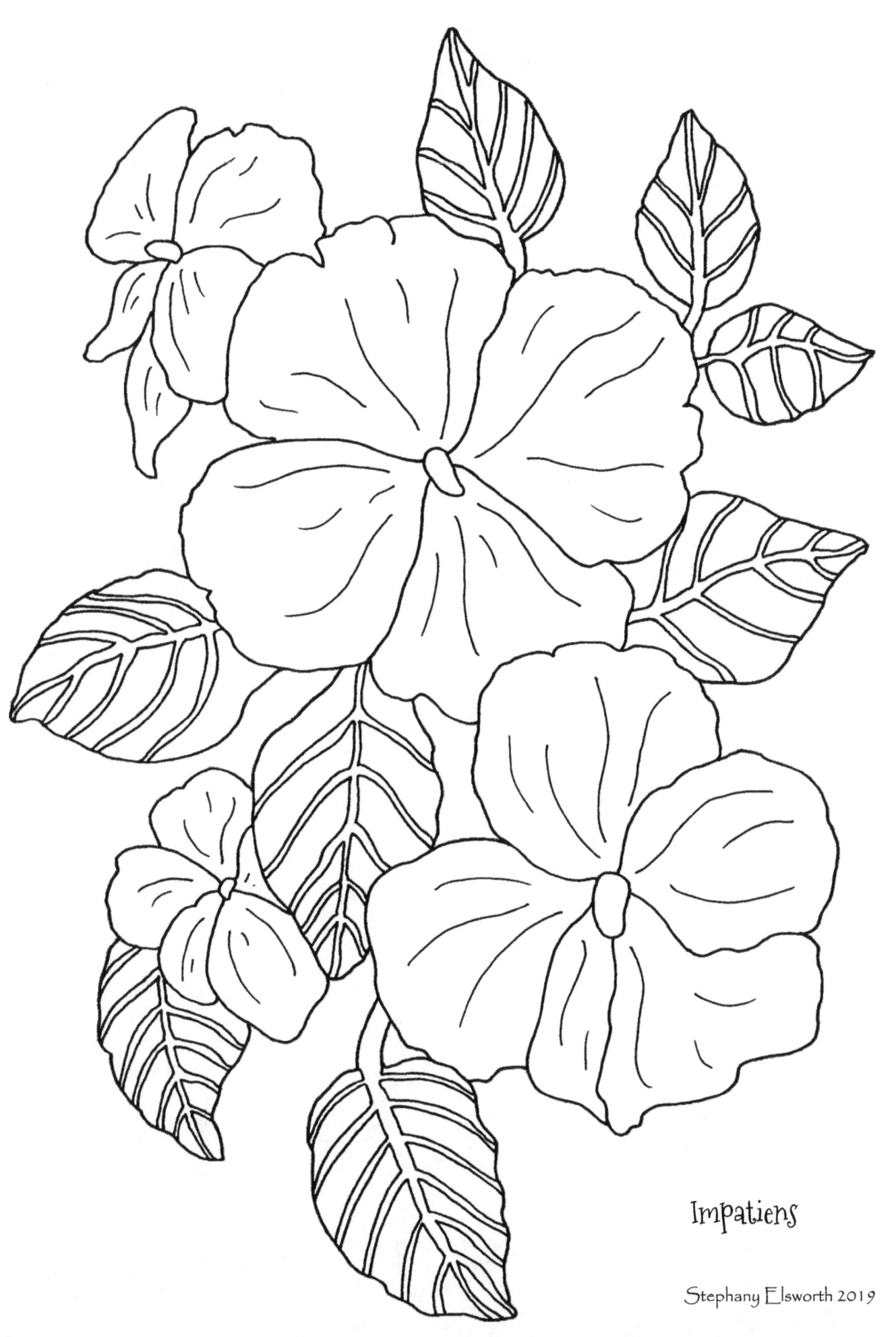

Impatiens

Stephany Elsworth 2019

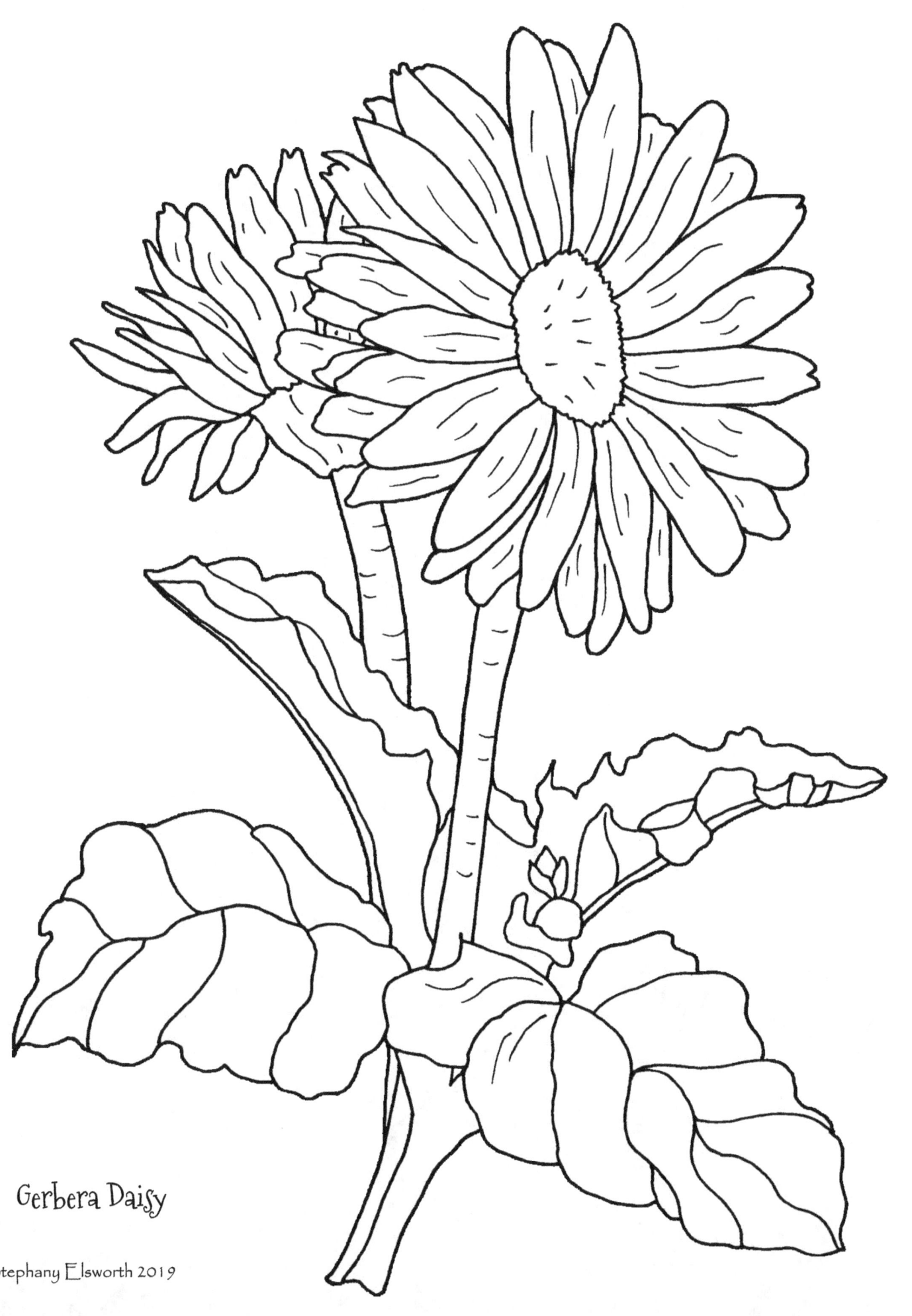

Gerbera Daisy

Stephany Elsworth 2019

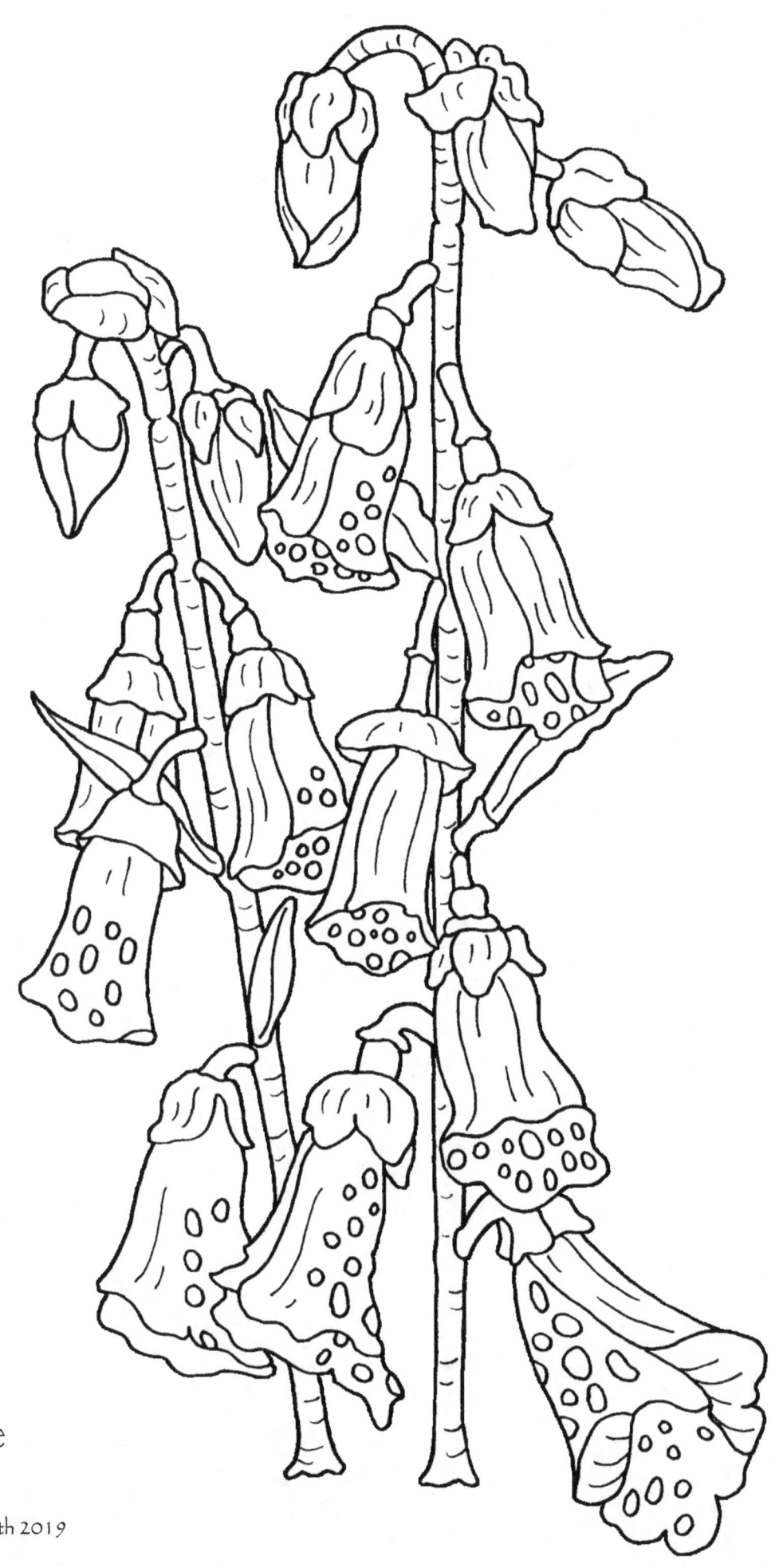

Foxglove

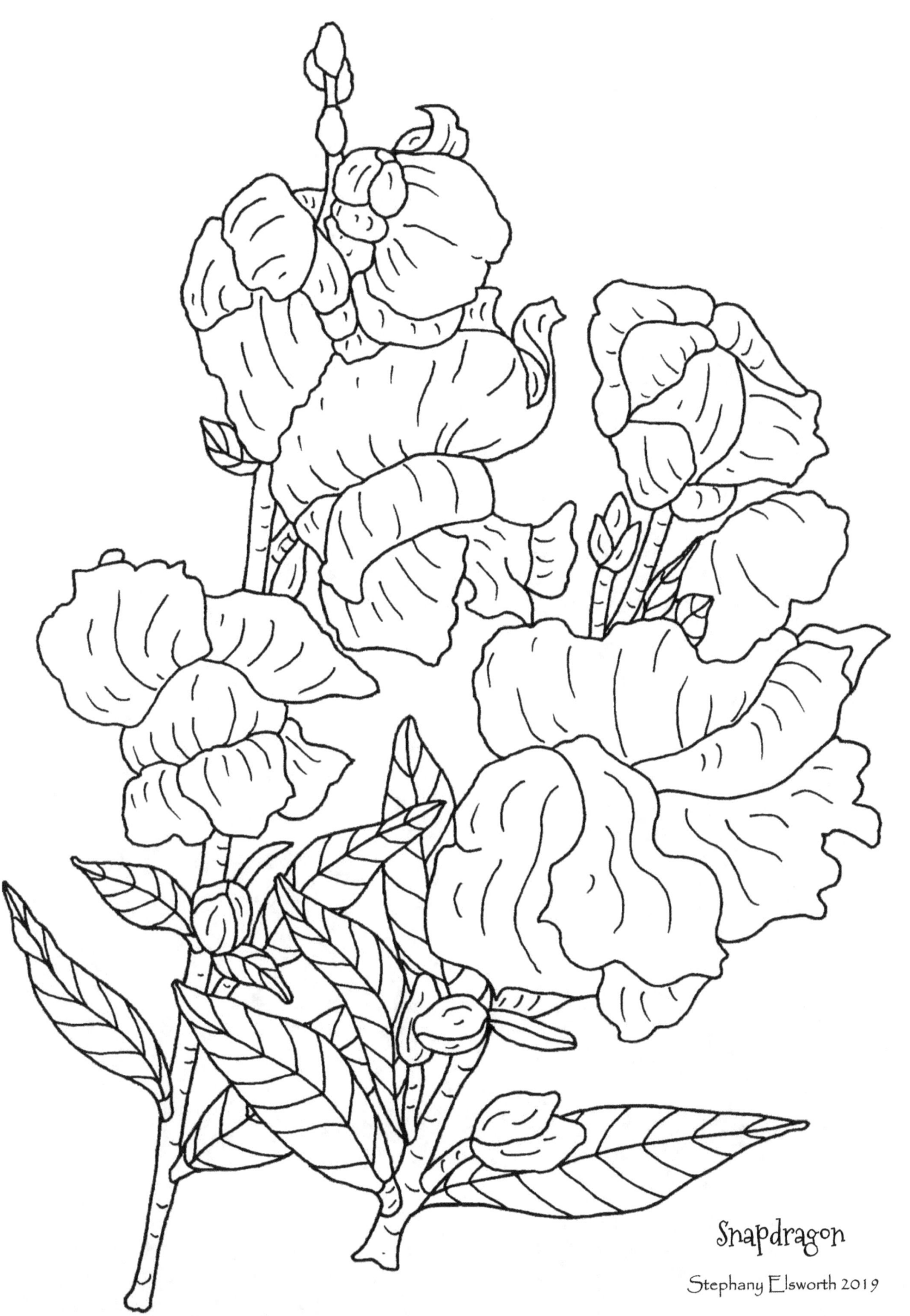

Snapdragon

Stephany Elsworth 2019

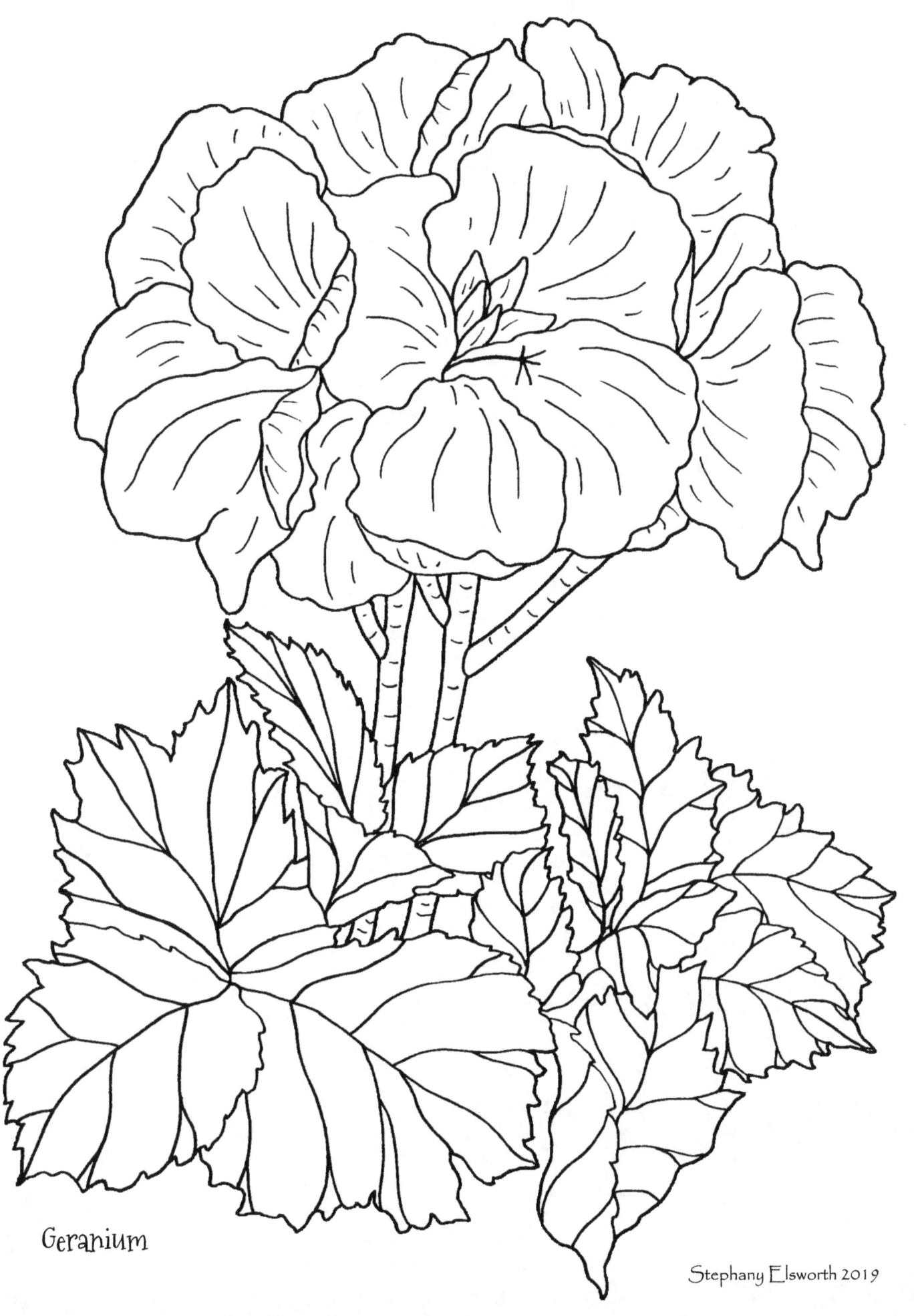

Geranium

Stephany Elsworth 2019

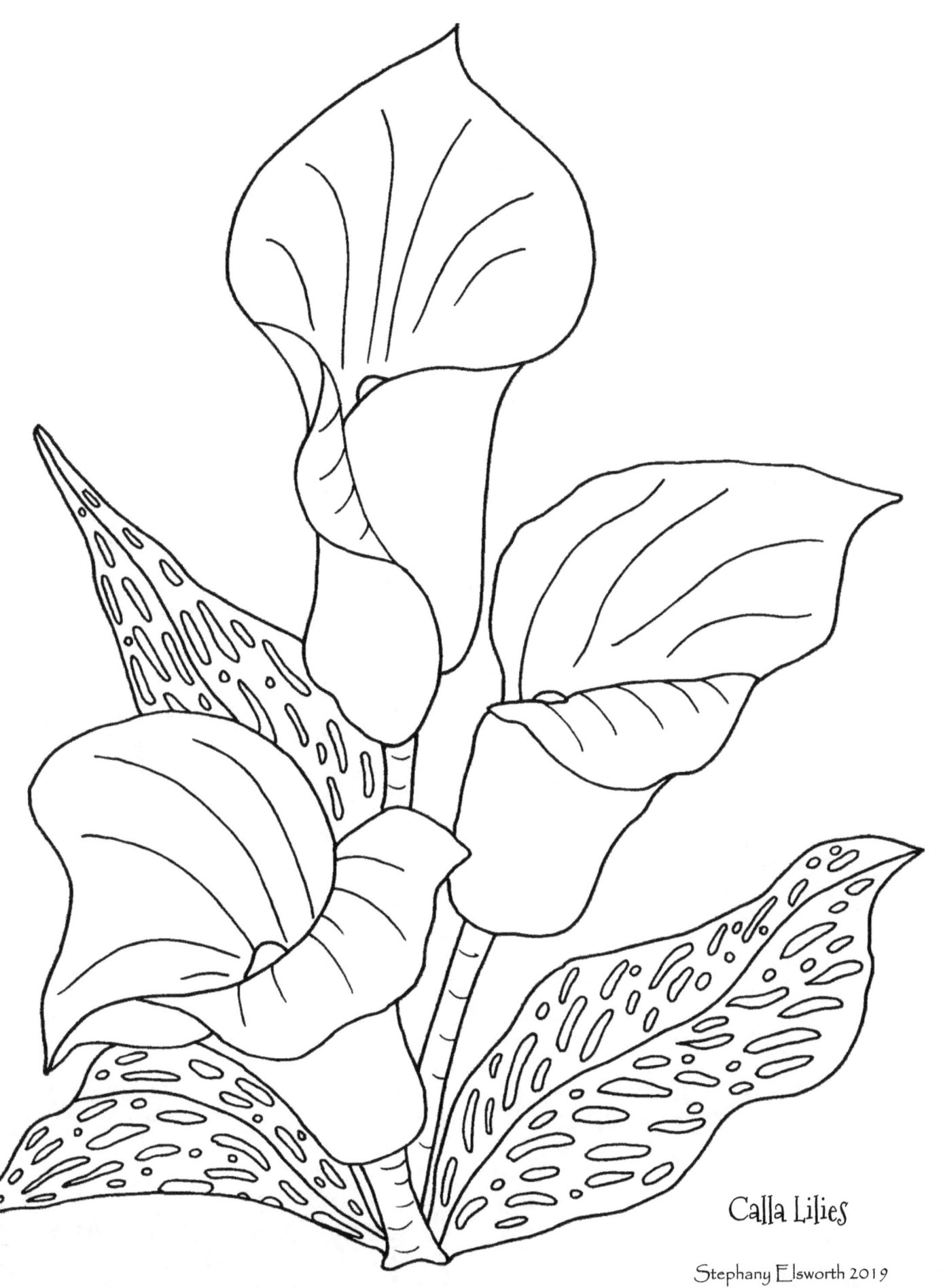

Calla Lilies

Stephany Elsworth 2019

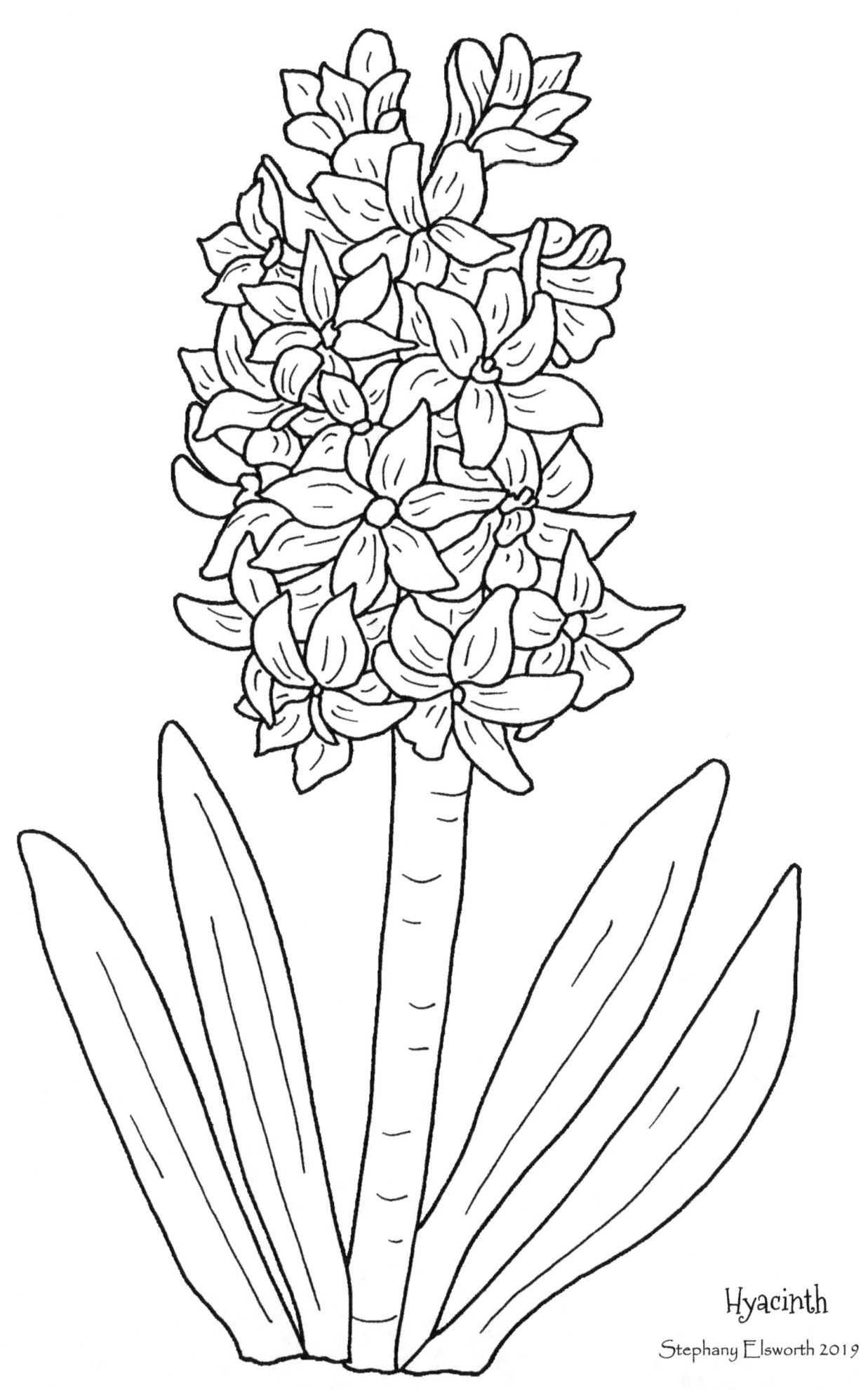

Hyacinth

Stephany Elsworth 2019

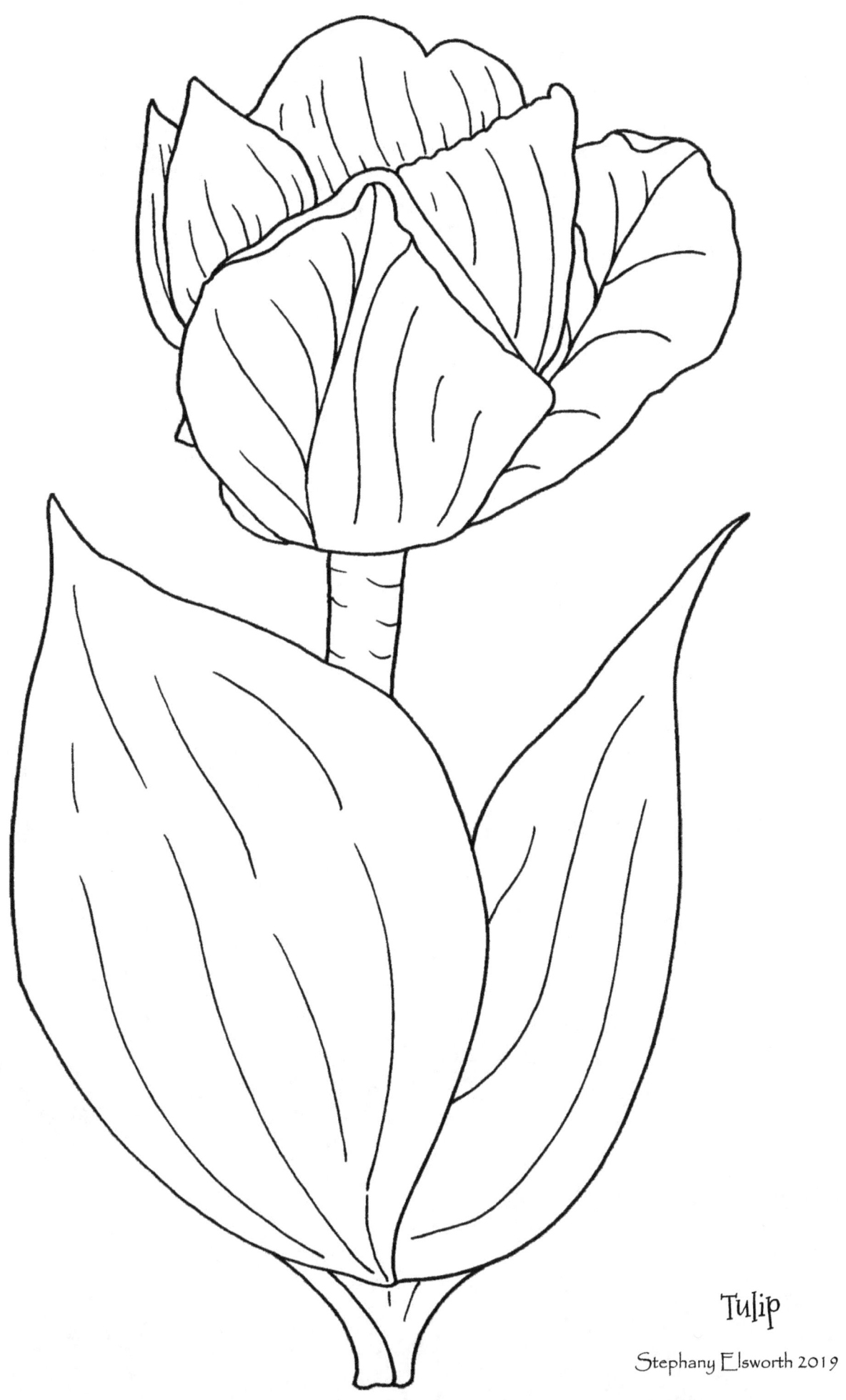

Tulip

Stephany Elsworth 2019

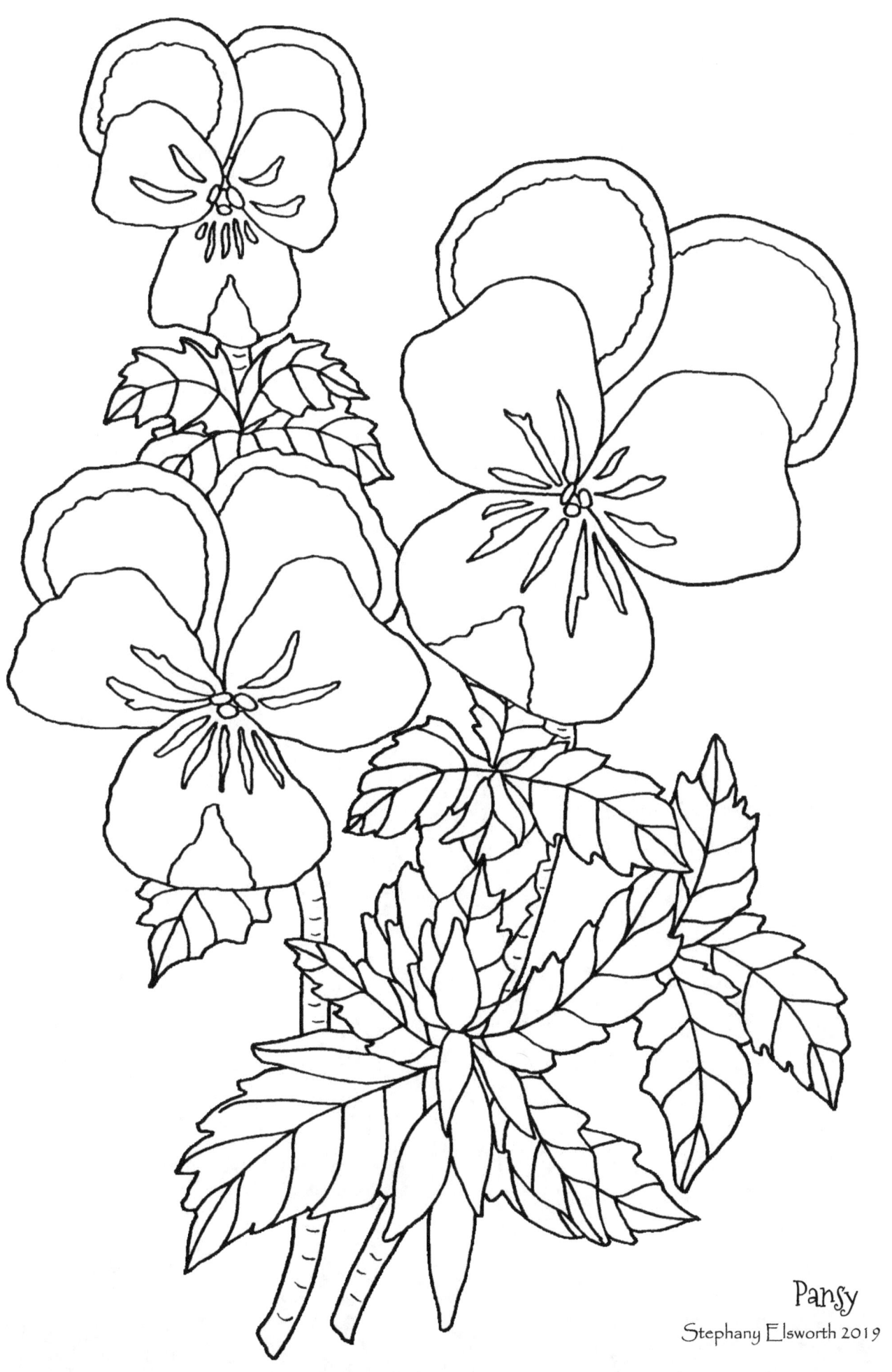

Pansy
Stephany Elsworth 2019

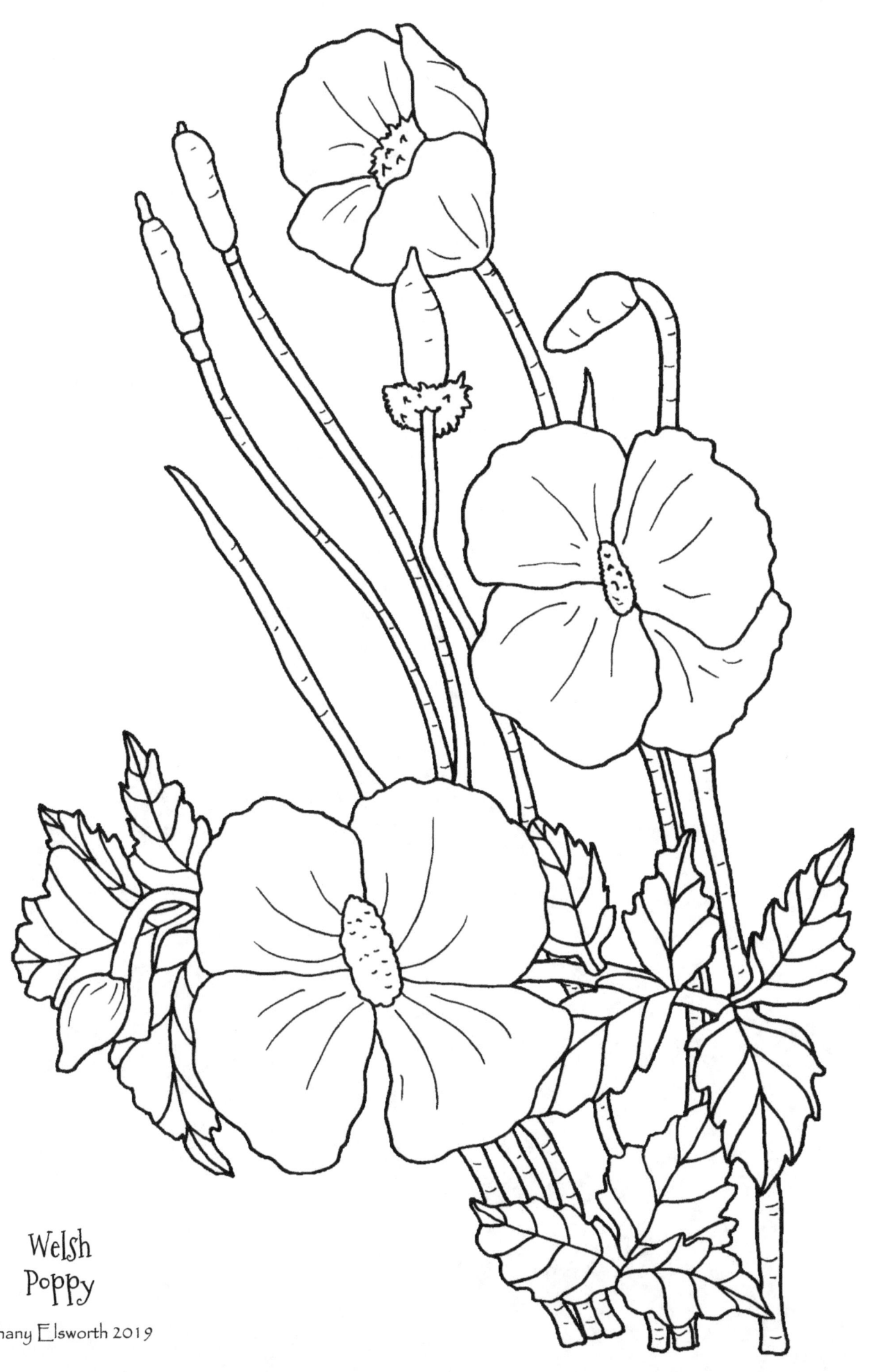

Welsh
Poppy

Stephany Elsworth 2019

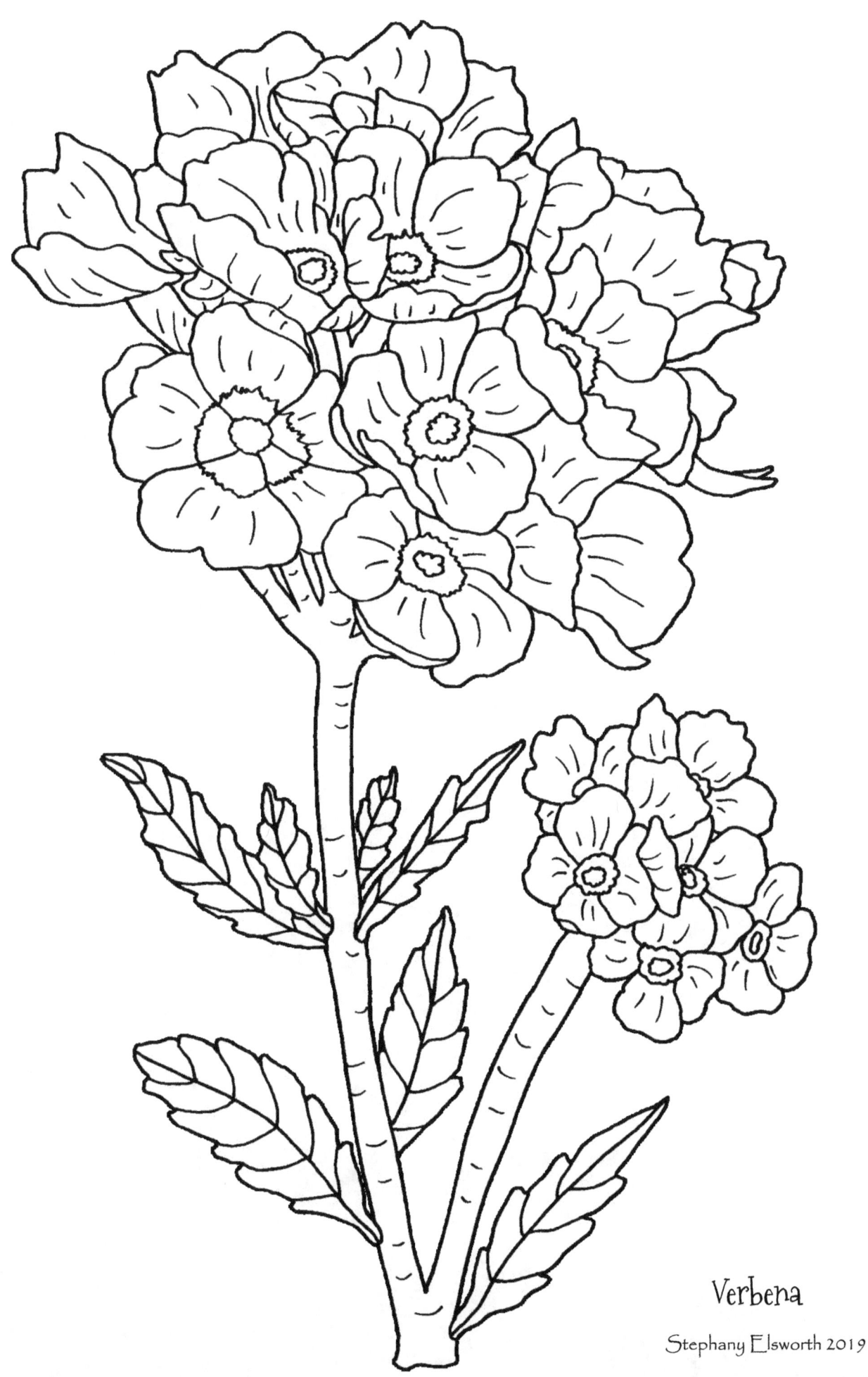

Verbena

Stephany Elsworth 2019

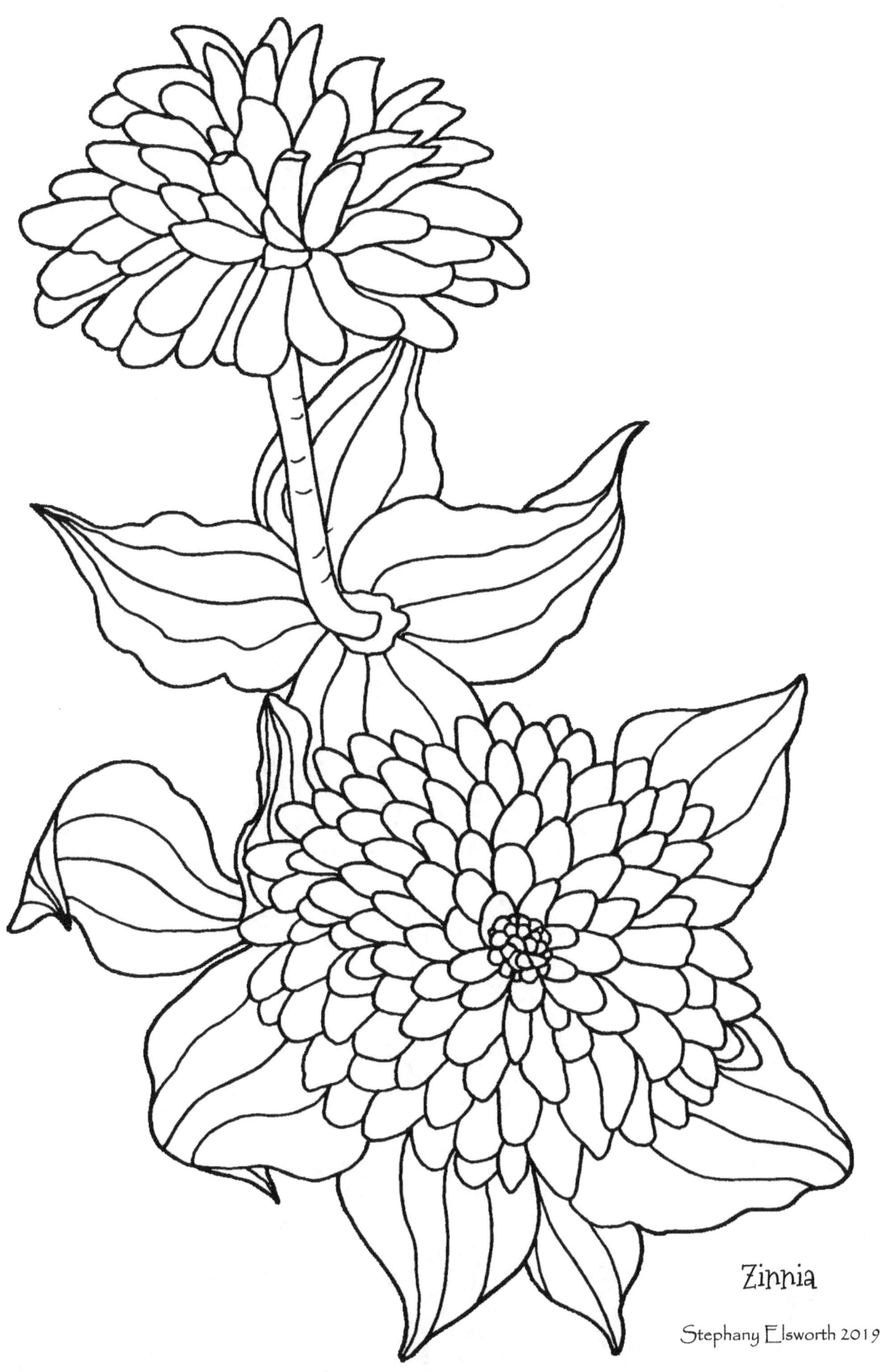

Zinnia

Stephany Elsworth 2019

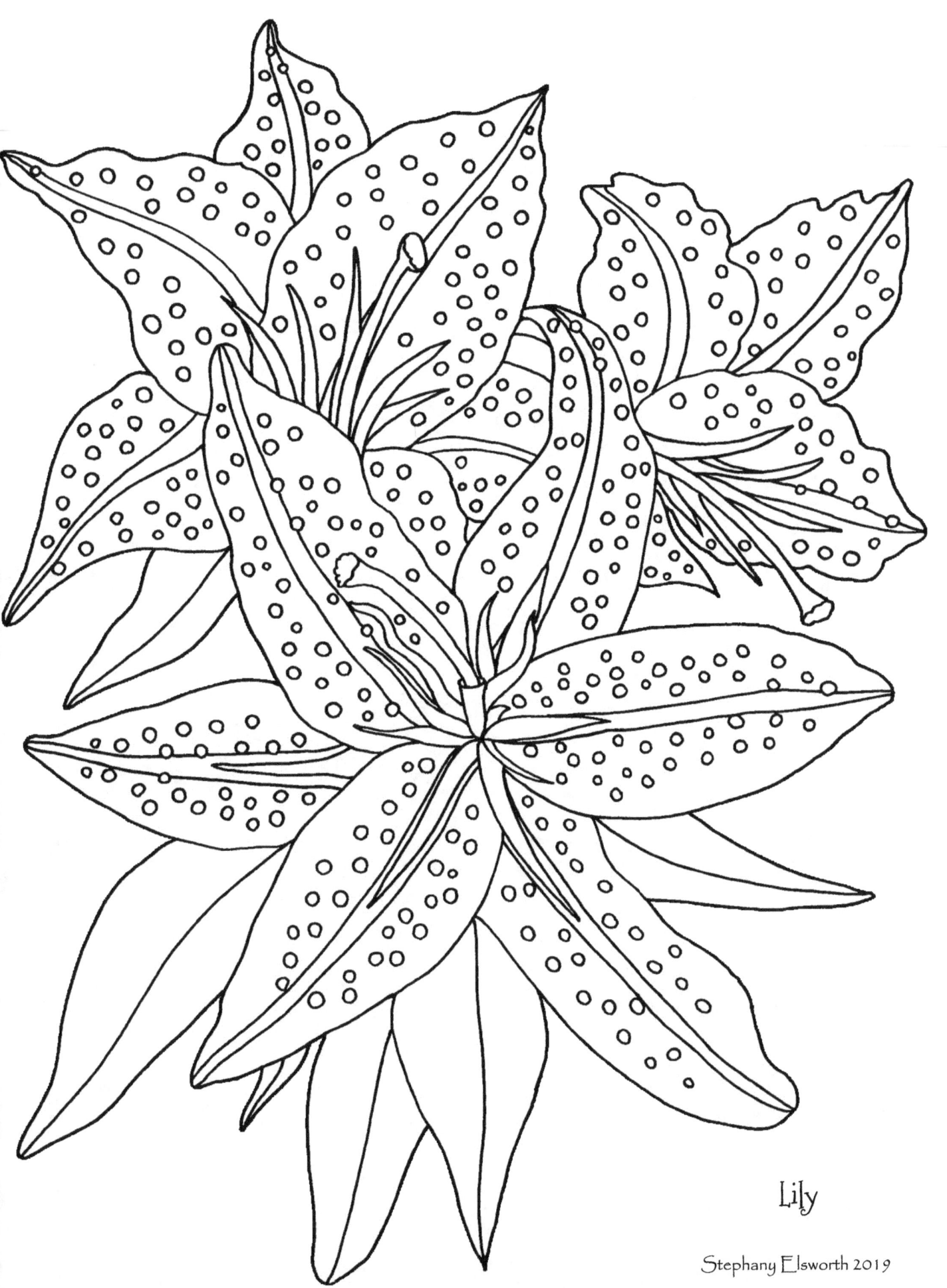

Lily

Stephany Elsworth 2019

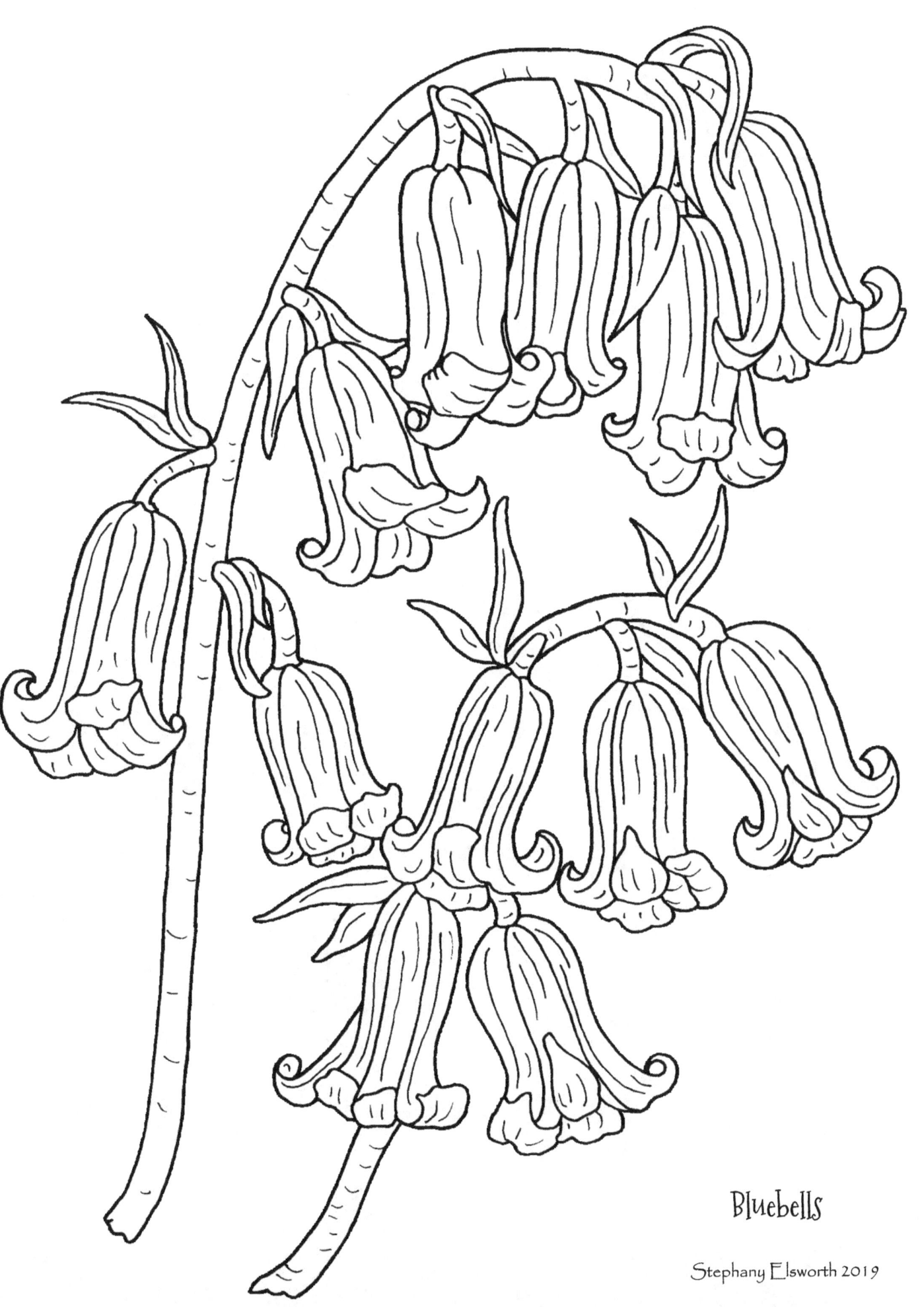

Bluebells

Stephany Elsworth 2019

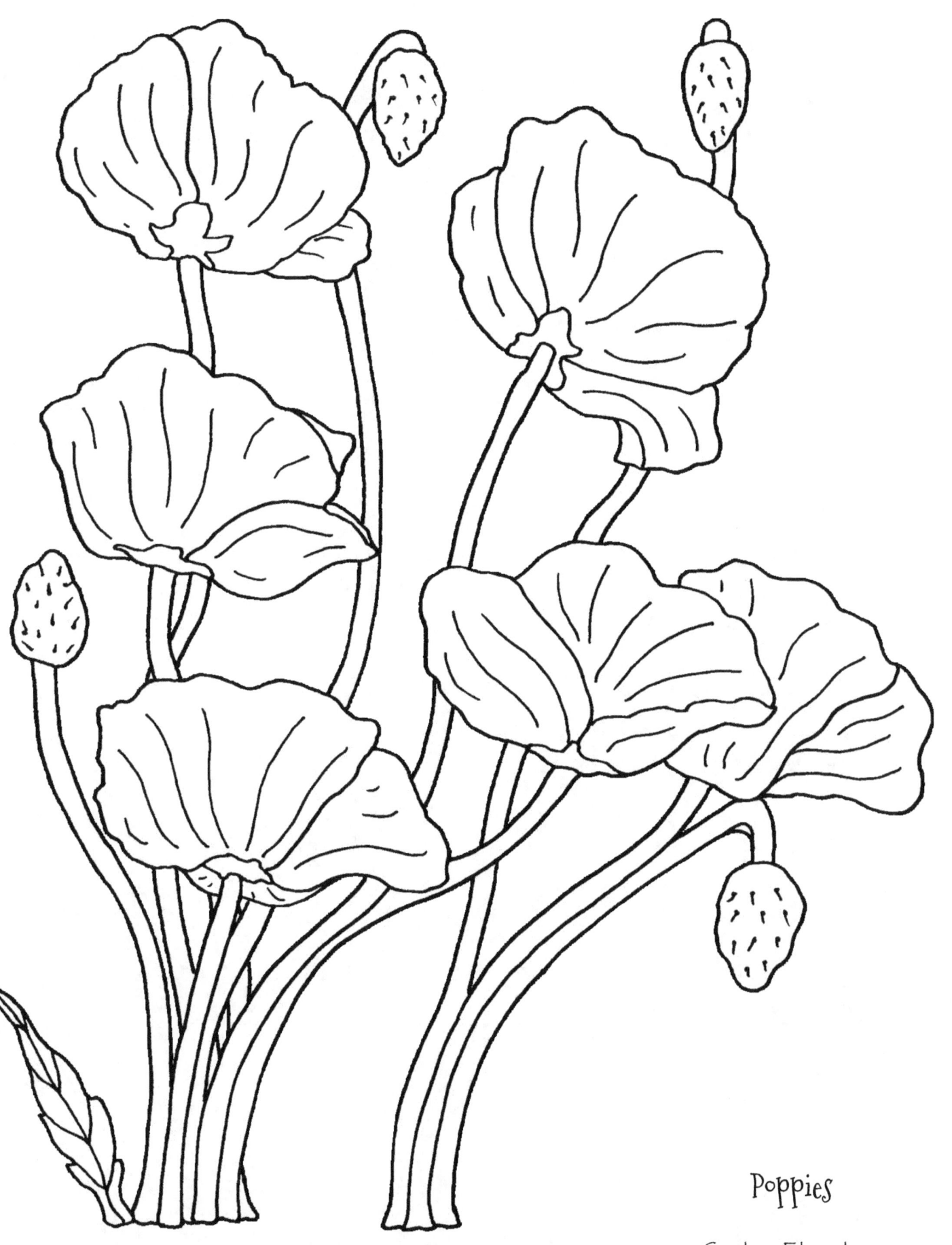

Poppies

Stephany Elsworth 2019

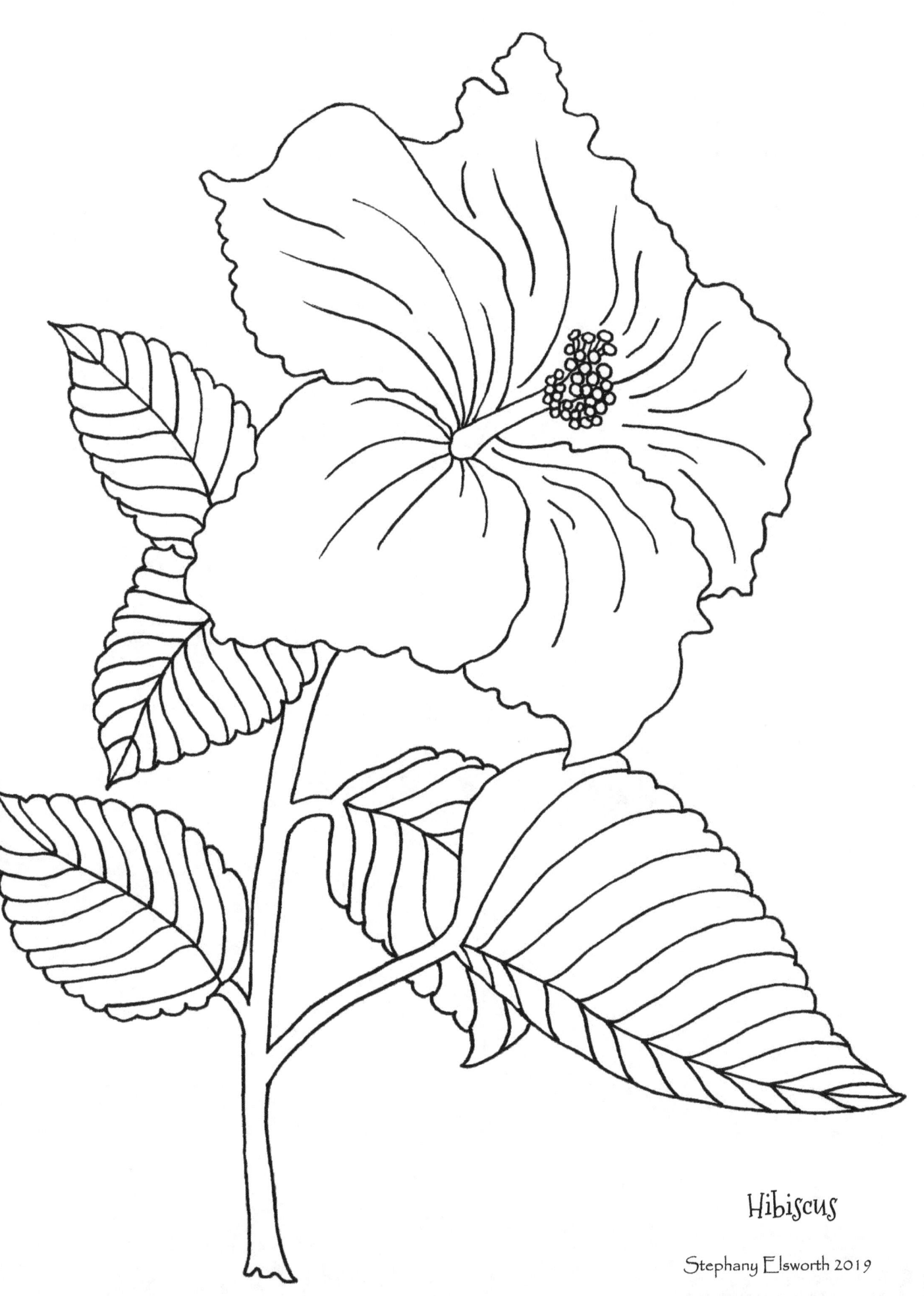

Hibiscus

Stephany Elsworth 2019